AF256151

Brush of Giftedness

Collection of original poetry and painted interpretations of art

Book and Poetry by Elizabeth Michele Cantine

Interpretations by Heidi Dong

DEDICATED

To those who recognize, appreciate, and inspire the giftedness in themselves and others…

To those with autism, Down syndrome, and challenges who create and recite poetry with

no words…

To those who dance to my poetry: Dahlia, Heidi, Dylan, Cole, Logan, and Holly

To those who realize that poetry and art will brush on forever…

CONTENTS

Introduction

This integration of arts collaboration is an extension of my "Well-Versed Artist Unit" from my many years as a classroom and fine arts educator. Every month, my class learned about a different artist, researching his/her life and selecting some recognized works. We practiced aesthetic scanning through role playing museum docent and visitor and read a picture as though we were reading a book. This was based on my training in discipline-based arts education from the Getty Institute. Then, the students would interpret the work through an art medium. Next, I composed a poem of critical analysis of the selected work and choreographed movements for each line of the verses. My students performed these poems for other classes, parents, and community groups. From these lessons, we became well-versed about the visual arts, could identify famous works of art, and would long remember these experiences implementing our multiple intelligences. For the video component of this book, young adult students with special needs, my Quotable Quartet, dance to the verses. They express the poetic words and the illustrated work implementing several genres of dance. Integration of the fine arts is the end product of the engaging process.

My motivation to embark on this current endeavor with artistic Heidi and the Quotable Quartet was to show that those with autism, Down syndrome, and other challenges do not need to vocalize – the arts validate their volumes of verses. Also, I wanted to share my poetry as a means of expression and enrichment. This book has been a career-long dream! I appreciate the many gifts and geniuses of past and present students, poets, and artists; I wish the world to see the ***Brush of Giftedness*** in everyone...

Thank you, Bradford, you've made your Mark!

Thank you, Bradford, you've made your Mark!
Gathering paper and other materials around your Leimert Park
                    Finding more than the tangible for your mural creations
                    Using memories from childhood and current events for inspirations
Affected by your wise mother and longtime work at her hair salon
Now it's your studio where you wash, dry, take down and set on

Lay**Layers** of paper, fabric, wood, paint, glue, and *String*
          Collage/ décollage, advertise/advocate, words/no words, - That's your thing!
You didn't need to be concerned about college classes or tuition
You are gifted with a "natural bent to intuition"
Plus definitely serious about theoretical education
        Abstraction/against abstraction – posters, ads, videos, huge walls of your commentary
        Paris, politics, power of media opinions you couldn't bury
*Pinocchio **is on** Fire* where we have to take more than a brief look
Your thought process and actual context would make a provocative book!
        Your combination of your life as a young black man, laws of patriarchy
        Seriously reflecting on the tragedy of Teddy Pendergrass with bias of hierarchy
None of this to be shattered or shamed
But a multimedia series to be studied and framed
        Your ***Helter Skelter*** selling for \$12 million plus more recognition and fame
        Highest price ever paid to a living African-American artist, now you're a real name!
                But money isn't your goal or dreams
                You want to show us life isn't what it seems
      We need to look around, look inside
      Into your passion and compassion, there's no free ride

Show it! Take a stand! In politics, masculinity, and cultural change
        Place it in your work, your thinking, and in the patterns you arrange
Abstract expressionism celebrated at the Wexner Center *As Panting* exhibition
Then the Wexner Center Residency Award in the Visual Arts, deserved recognition!
        With lead support by the Andy Warhol Foundation for the Visual Arts
        Your pieces considered as paintings without brush or pallet to compose the parts
Live within, work within from whatever home = a bond
Community is Art, organic feelings, working alone, we respond…
As we admire the creative context you display in South-Central LA
        What is disputed, discarded, and deflected can be refuted, regarded, and respected
        Your gathered papers and bits create **stratum**, images, and ideas reflected
Now 10 canvases hung at the Broad – ***Big Blue*** Watts map with no middle of the road
        You make us think, react, and see obscurities out of the dark
        Thank you, Bradford, you've made your Mark!

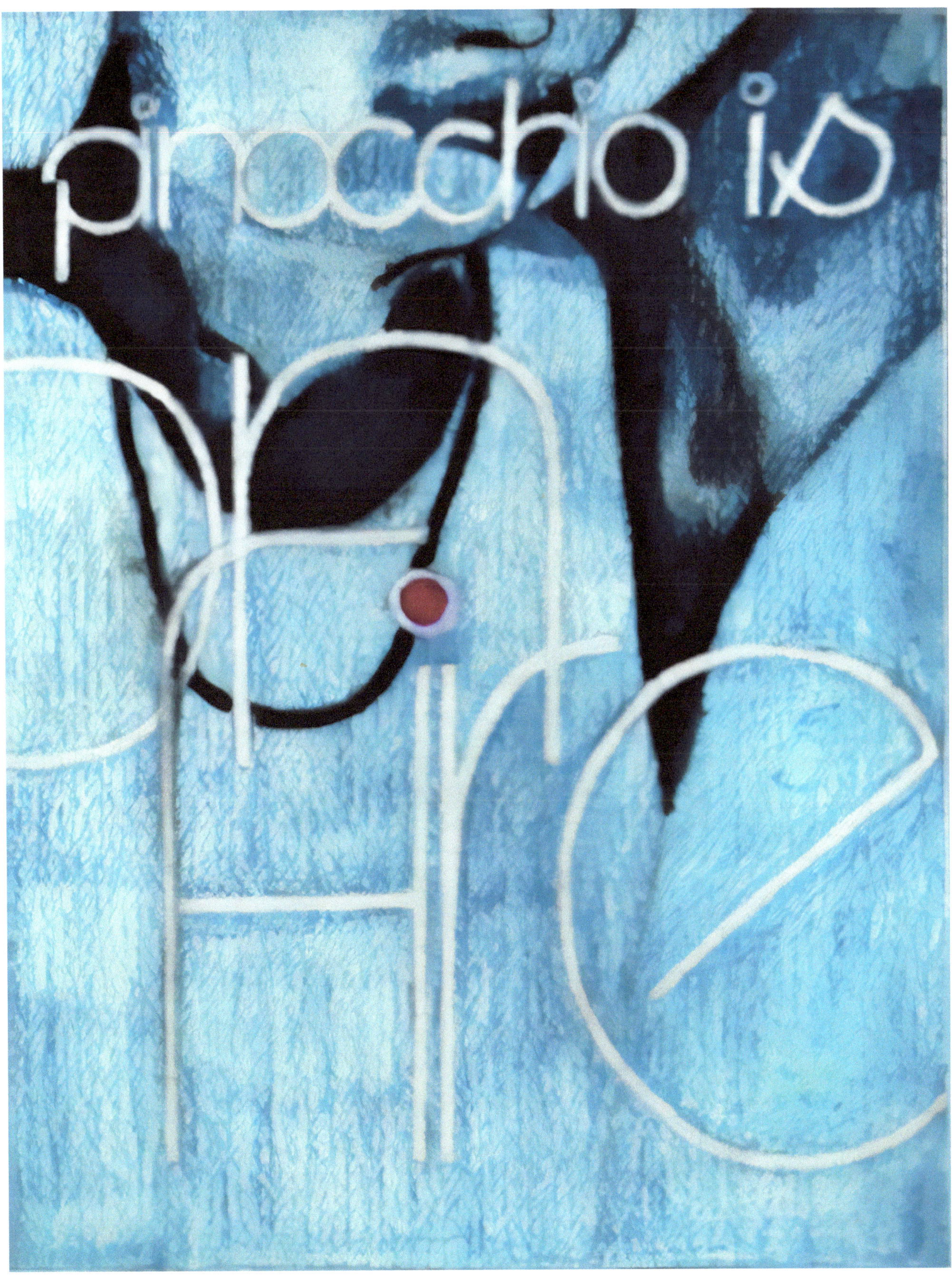

pinocchio io

Mary Cassatt Painted *Child in a Straw Hat*

Let's think about that…

Mary Cassatt painted ***Child in a Straw Hat***
Let's think about that…
She painted many others
Of children and their mothers
And ***Children Playing on the Beach***
What peacefulness they teach
When painting was not a popular female occupation
She made a strong statement for women's liberation!
Ignoring her family wishes, she studied in Europe
and admired Japanese prints
Influencing her soft style from these artistic tints
Although she was born in Pittsburgh, PA,
She often lived in Paris, France,
Where her friend Degas painted her and the ballet
dance

There, the acclaimed Degas and Manet mentored her
In 1879, she joined the Impressionists and their
allure
Another unpopular venture for sure!
She used bold lines and flat colors in the
Impressionistic way
To then become the most famous woman painter in
the U.S.A
She introduced Impressionism to the U.S. making
the connection
Plus earning respect as art consultant to Havemeyer
collection
Later France's Legion of Honor in 1904
Sadly, blindness prevented her from doing more
Mary Cassatt painted "Child in a Straw Hat"
Let's think about that…

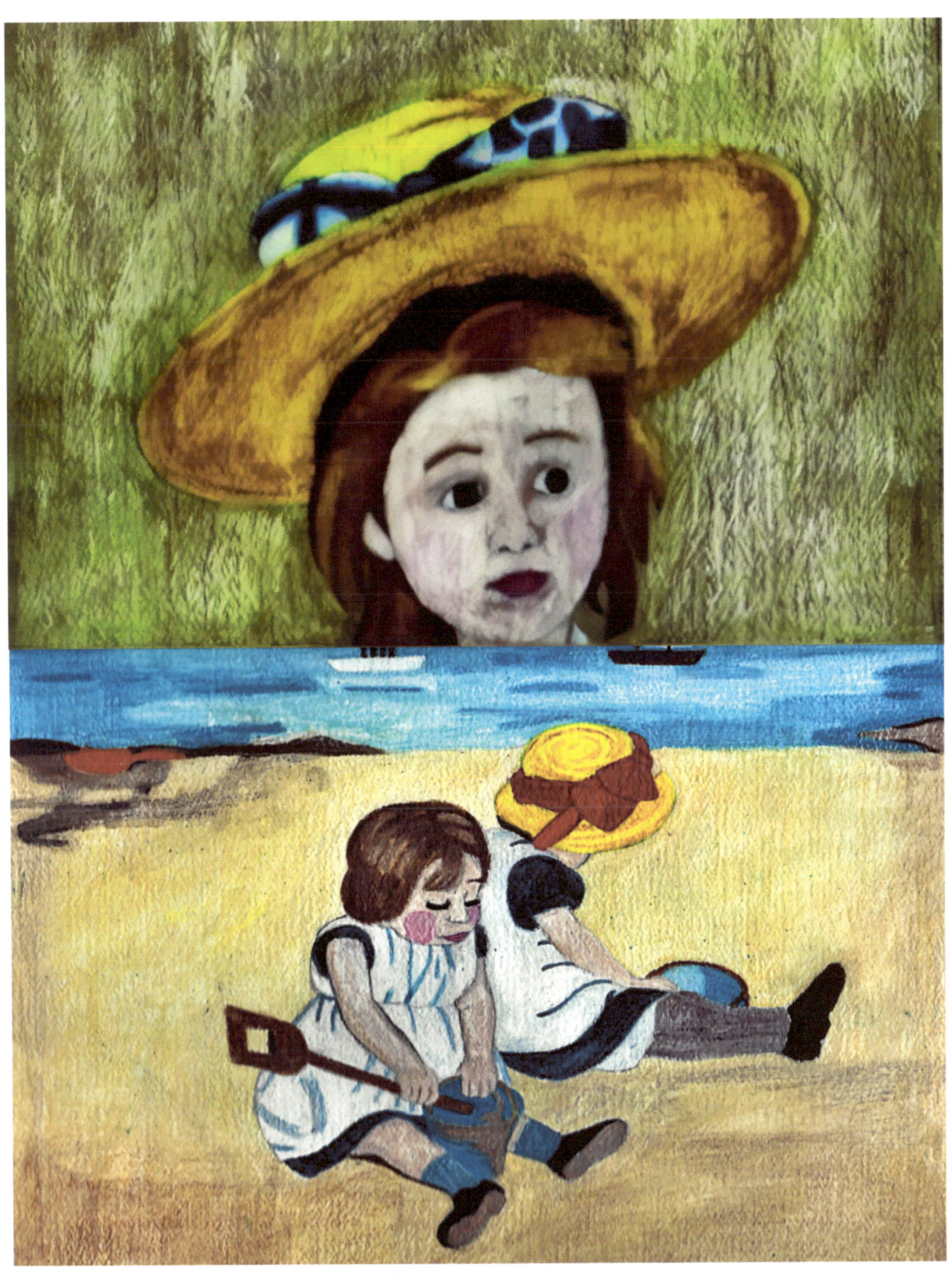

Chagall, Chagall, you loved it all!

Subjects **flying**, floating   upside down   on your canvas, on your mind

From your village Vitebsk and everywhere surreal stories of every kind
       Recalling Jewish Proverbs and Russian folk tales
       Mapping your beloved childhood memory trails

Imaginative, creative, colorful **whimsy**
Pathed in modern metaphor, in dreams, in fantasy
Your individualism, humanism, imaginative heart
       Love of home, Paris, and people sets you apart
       You studied in Paris, inspired and learned from experiencing the city
You returned home with no worry, shame, or pity
       World War I began you could not leave

So why not paint everything in which you believe?
Bible, family, friends, animals, trees and flowers
Sixty paintings then, who's counting the hours?
Animals, lovers and angels, a fiddler on the roof
I thought he was just a musical theater lead, alone and aloof

       But you placed him **high**, he's immortalized
       Your admiration of your favorite uncle, a violinist, is realized
Myriad mysteries and mélange in each canvas centimeter
       In *The Birthday* painting for your beloved Bella a bouquet does greet her
       Love was everything to you; as you ask us only to love you
How can we not be enamored with your work in each medium?
Stained glass windows, sculptures, ballet sets, theater tapestries on and on without tedium

       Le Cirque your **circus** lithographs and introspective text
       Feelings for performers and animals – the show is over, what's next?
Reflecting on their lives and audience excitement in every town
Empathizing with each entertainer - the terror of the tiger, the tear of the clown
       We yearn to interpret the verse of each thing and each thought

       Your poetry in creative style, in **fascination** we're caught
Two huge murals calling out to us at the Met

More to say, more to do – at 97 you weren't done yet!
More to see such as your recent display At the exquisite ***Boston's Galerie d'Orsay***

Marc Chagall, dream **up** don't **fall** you loved it all!

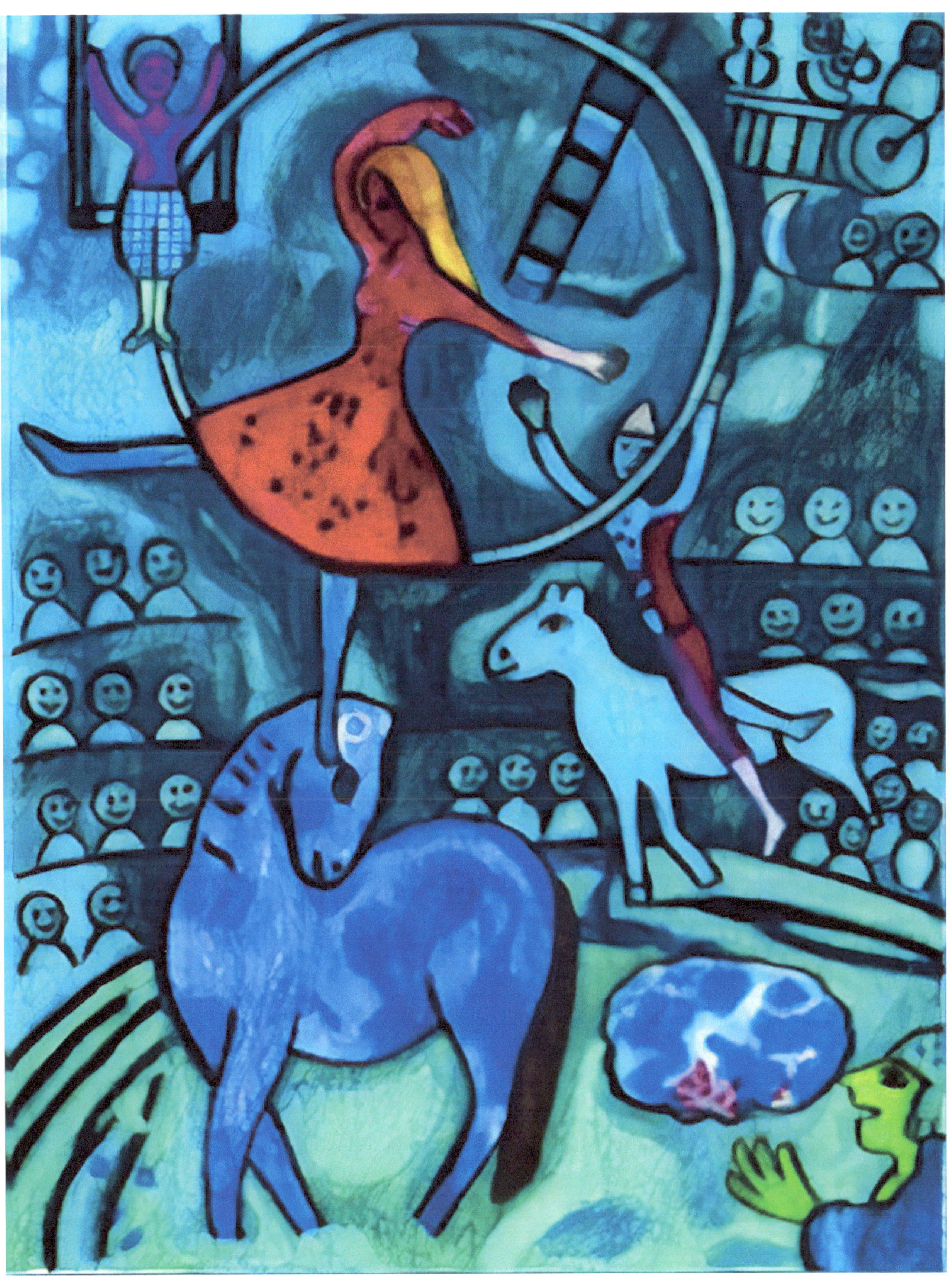

Leonardo da Vinci from Vinci from Italy!

Leonardo da Vinci

from Vinci from Italy!

(Tarantella, pizza, and spaghetti)

He studied the body, that's called anatomy

Used math in his sketchings and his paintings, ah—

The most famous of which is the **Mona Lisa**, actually named **La Gioconda**

The pyramid and delicate form, those eyes, that intriguing smile, and colors warm

But da Vinci was a scientist, to boot! Water skis, armored car, flying machine, and parachute!

His brilliant mind dazzles us (Did he know Christopher Columbus?)

Leonardo da Vinci from Vinci from Italy

A genius, a genius, a genius!

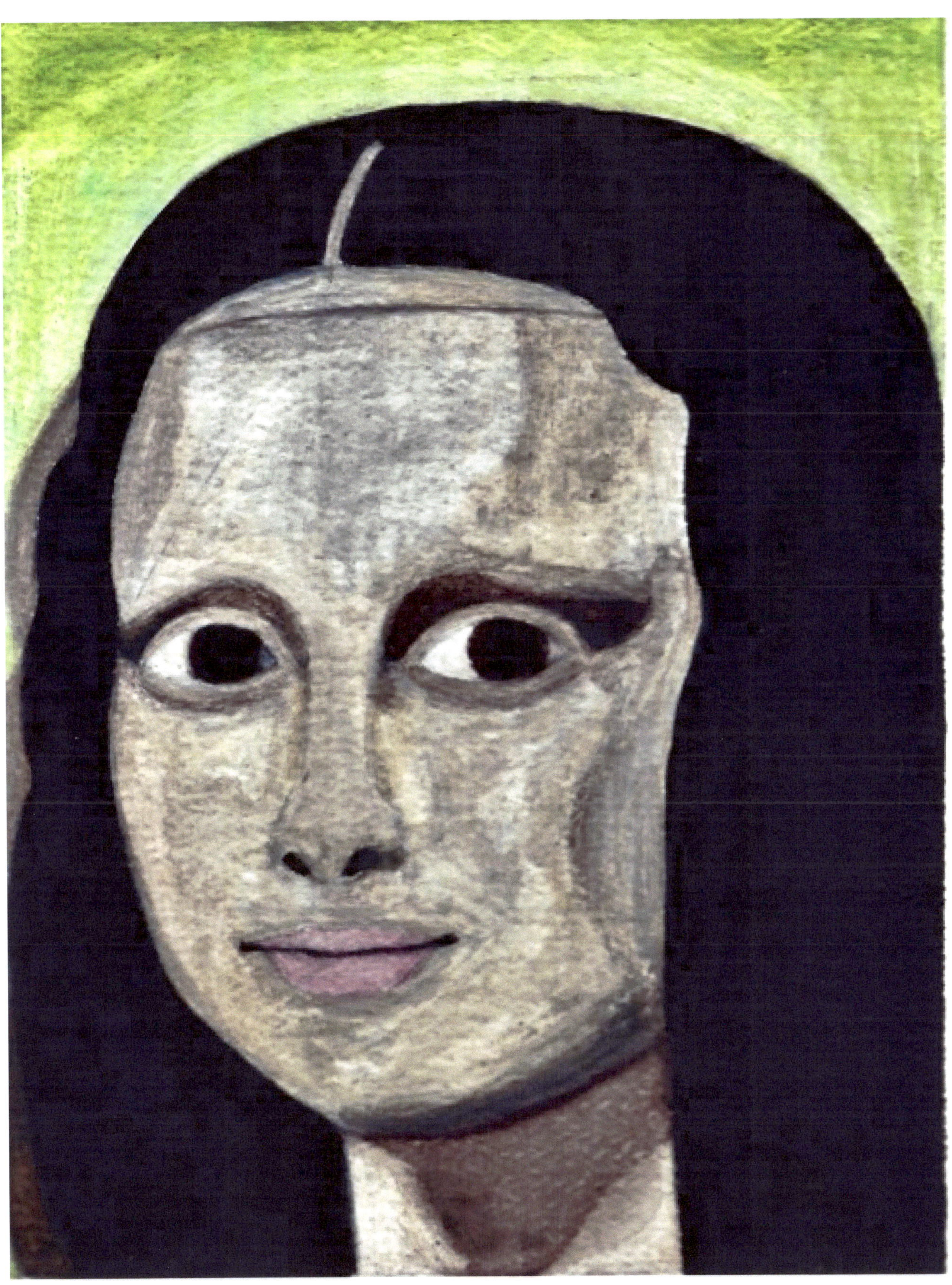

Degas, Degas, C'est Magnifique!

Degas, Degas, c'est magnifique, n'est-ce pas?

Vive la France! Vive la danse!

Degas painted many scenes of the ballet dance

He captured the dancers' form and their stance

Concentrated on the body's lines, movements, and natural pose

Sometimes relaxed, sometimes on toes

Striving for balance and composition

He sculpted ballerinas in fourth position

Molding figures in wax and clay

He painted in a somewhat impressionistic way

But his style was uniquely his own

Inspired by Italian masters and Japanese tone

So he could better create he lived alone

Though friends included Cassatt, Manet, Van Gogh, and Monet

Whom he influenced by his racetracks, circuses, theatre, and ballet

Degas, Degas, c'est magifique, n'est-ce pas?

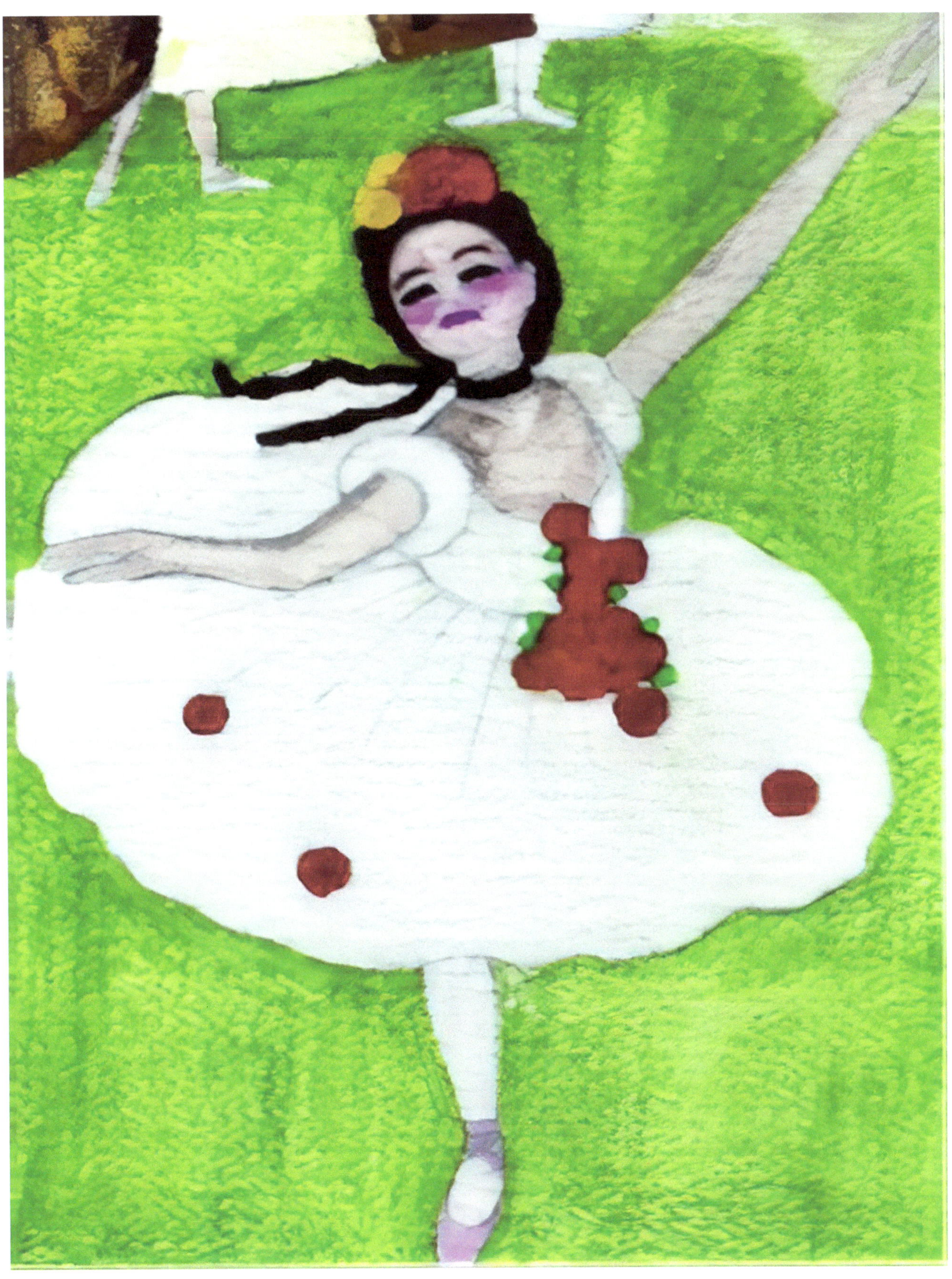

Winslow Homer Loved the sea and the shore

Winslow Homer loved the sea and the shore
Winslow Homer painted boats and much more

He illustrated battles of the Civil War
He also painted farm and country lore

He visited Paris and the London coast
Deciding he liked harbors the most

Returning to the United States
Prout's Neck, Maine, suited his taste

He lived alone with Sam his dog
He studied nature, light, clouds and fog

Visited Bermuda, showed us Nassau
He painted exactly what he saw

Realism was the style the old master did frame
Snap the Whip was a children's game

Lone sailor on **The Gulf Stream** fears no shark
Though we feel afraid in the waves in the dark…

Winslow Homer loved the sea and the shore
Winslow Homer painted boats and much more

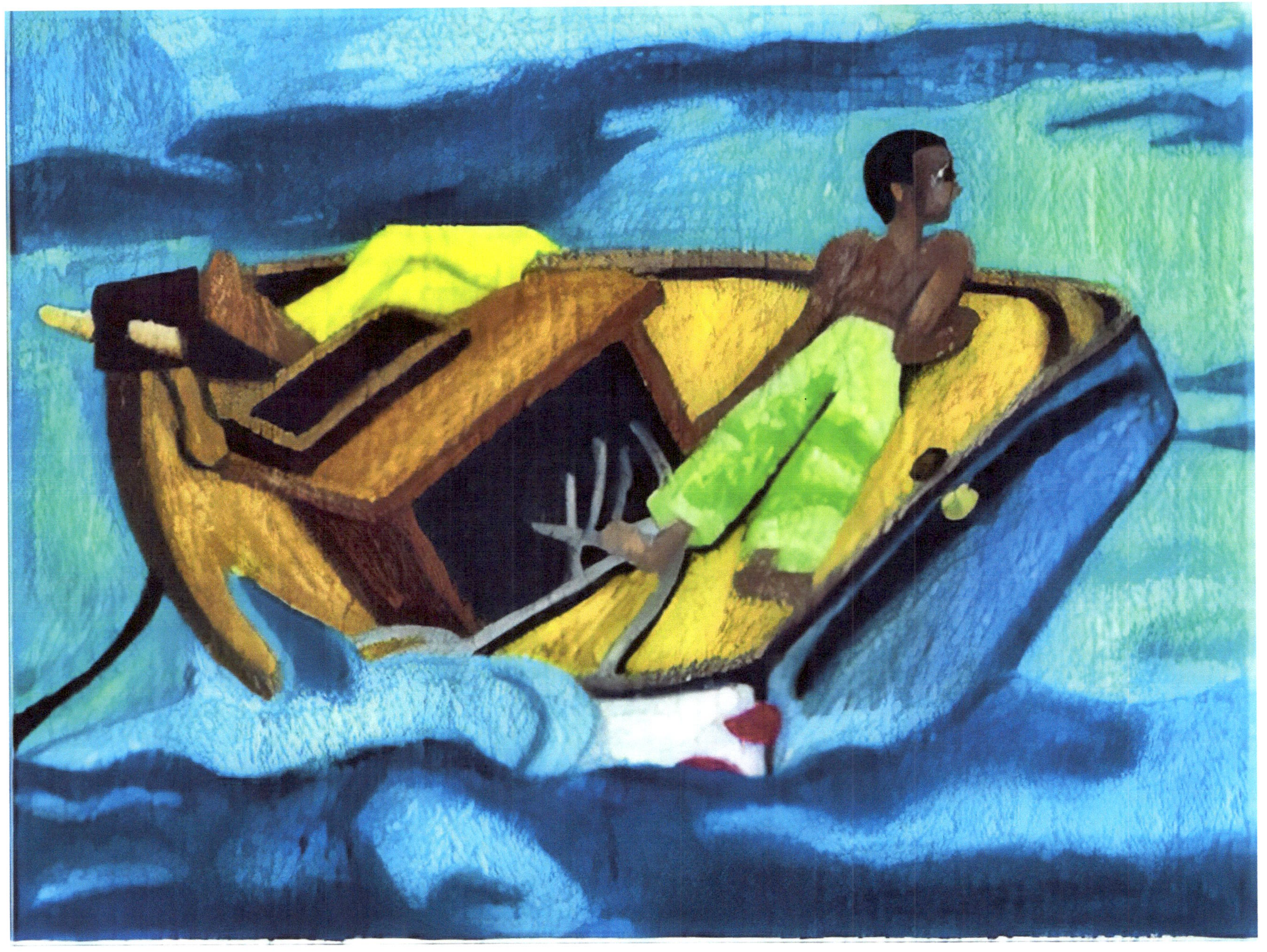

¡Viva la Vida! ¡Viva la Frida!

¡Viva la Vida! ¡Viva la Frida!
Hear us chant, hear us shout

But you only heard your voice so many days in and out
Of your beloved blue house where you were born, blossomed, then withered
Where your stubborn spirit never quivered
With a lifetime of illnesses and injuries defied!
Battling polio as a child with your resolve ratified
So the "Peg Leg" teasing pushed you to your Papa's photography
And to wear pants and long skirts to hide your deformity
Then a terrible bus accident left you again broken
But not down for long, not by any token!
Borrowing your dad's prized brushes and paints
Lying on your back now creativity replaced constraints
You would become a painter instead of a doctor
Then a superb teacher, mentor, and proctor
Photographic memory, artist, linguist, promoter of Mexican culture
Revered and respected artist and sculptor
Wearable art - Mexican fashionista!
Toda Bella - ¡Bella Vista!
We agree you were a work of art
You are a colorful, traditional work of art!
Over half of your pieces are self portraits - How appropriately smart!
Your bushy eyebrows, never smiling solemn lips
Since your beauty had to endure severe hardships
Coping with setbacks, divorce and remarriage to daunting Diego
Attraction and distraction with your famous amigo
Who recognized your genius and smiled at your tricks
Your innate naughtiness that you displayed just for kicks!
You had some great times together though you kept your own name
The Louvre admired and purchased your painting of *The Frame*
What serious recognition of your talents and fame!
But then more operations and debilitating pain
In later years painting still lifes to mirror the stillness in your body
Hosting your first solo exhibit in Mexico impassioned, not haughty
You set up your bed in the gallery without any doubt
You were living every moment until time, too soon ran out...

Now with worldwide and wild acclaim we chant and shout
¡Viva la Vida! ¡Viva la Frida!

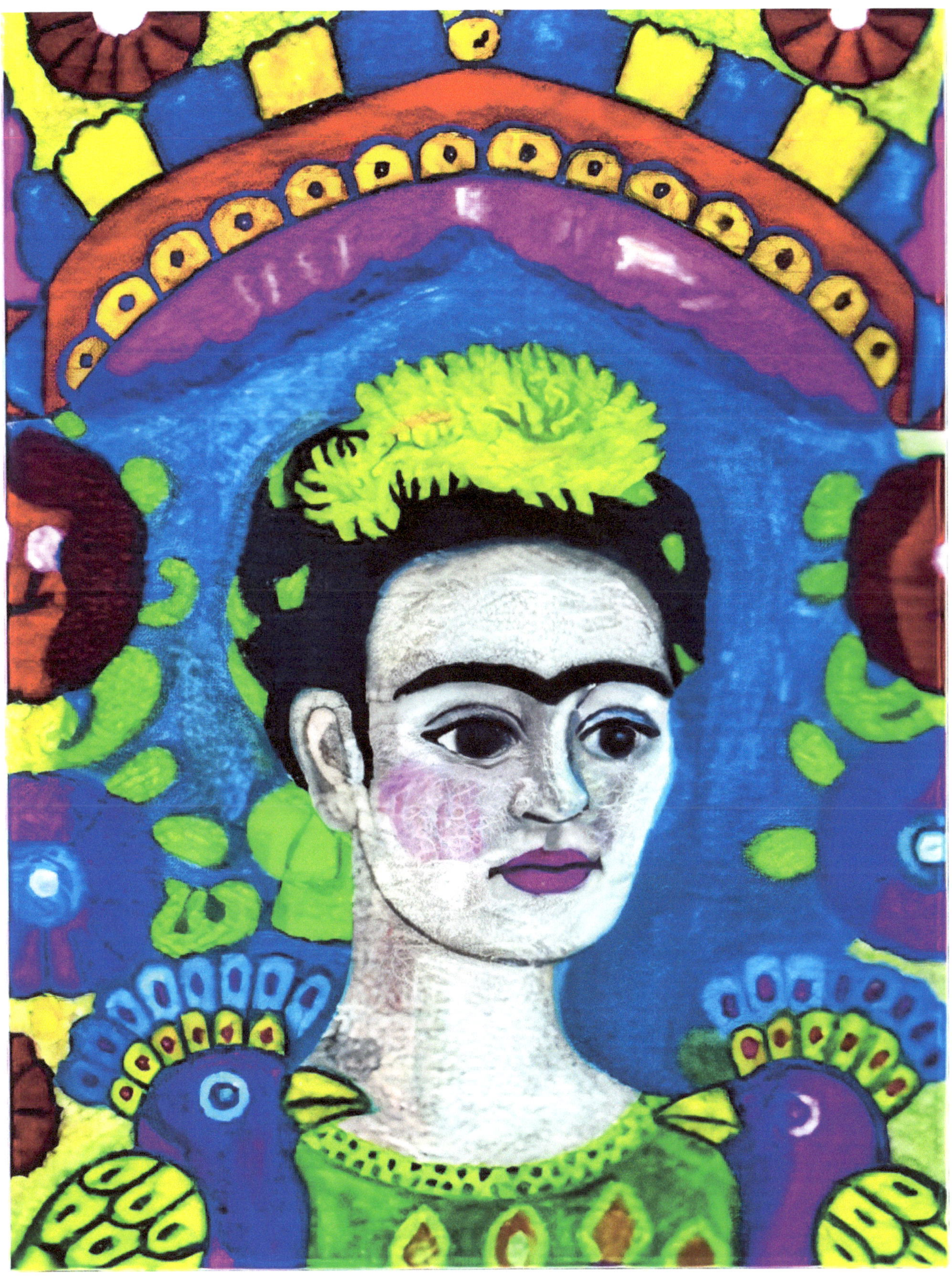

Monster (Fauve) Matisse

Bo be da do wa
Monster Matisse
Bo be da do wa
He made things with these
Illustrator, painter, patterns, pizzazz
He published a book and called it *JAZZ*

Cut it out,

cut it out
Colors that shout!
Feelings, stories, people in time
Icarus falling, bright bursts calling
Seaweed wreathing, rhythm breathing
Circuses, horses, dagger throwers, too
Cut it out,

cut it out
Don't feel blue

Before his illness, he could hold a brush
To paint figures, still lifes, interior scenes
Intense colors, unusual extremes
Illustrate books using just a few lines

Simple faces, flowers without vines

Bo be da do wa
Monster Matisse
Bo be da do wa
He made things with these
Illustrator, painter, patterns, pizzazz
He published a book and called it *JAZZ*

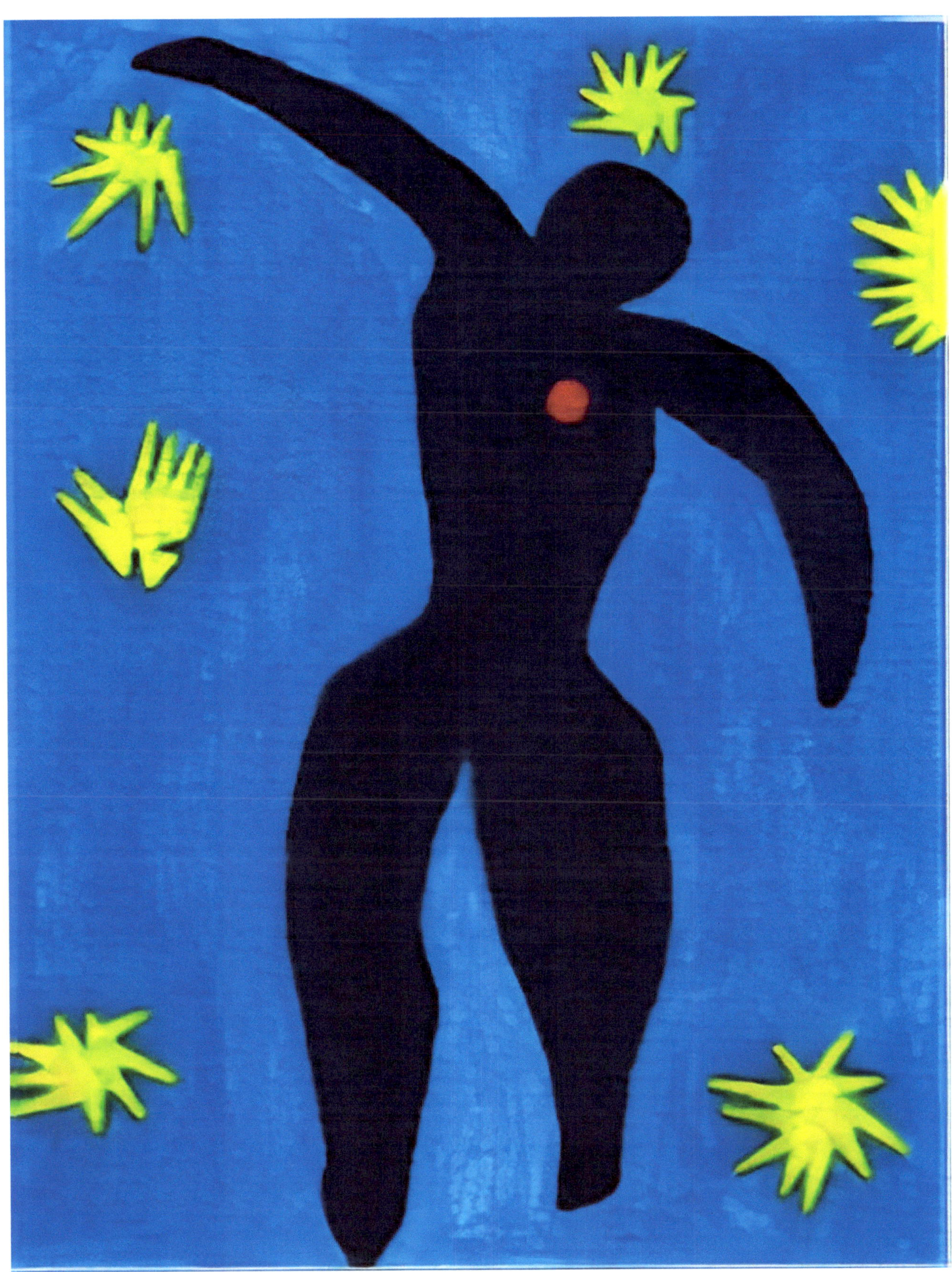

Where's Monet Today?

Where's Monet today?
Outdoors in France, in Impressionism
That's where you'll find him

Outdoors, Monet, you studied light
To paint your Impression: Sunrise just right

Reflecting off the water is a small, orange sun
Your background of warm colors shows us day has begun

No details on the boats, just patches of black
Textures show motion forward and back

From this one work, a critic is disdain, called all your work **"Impressionist"**
And gave the movement its name

You observed changes in light and atmosphere
Painting your subject somewhat unclear

But we can see your Water Lilies
Though you were almost **blind**
Not as lilies really are
But as an **abstract** *kind*

These flowers inspired others to paint that way
So you were a leader then, and today?

Where's Monet today?
Outdoors in France, in Impressionism
That's where you'll find him

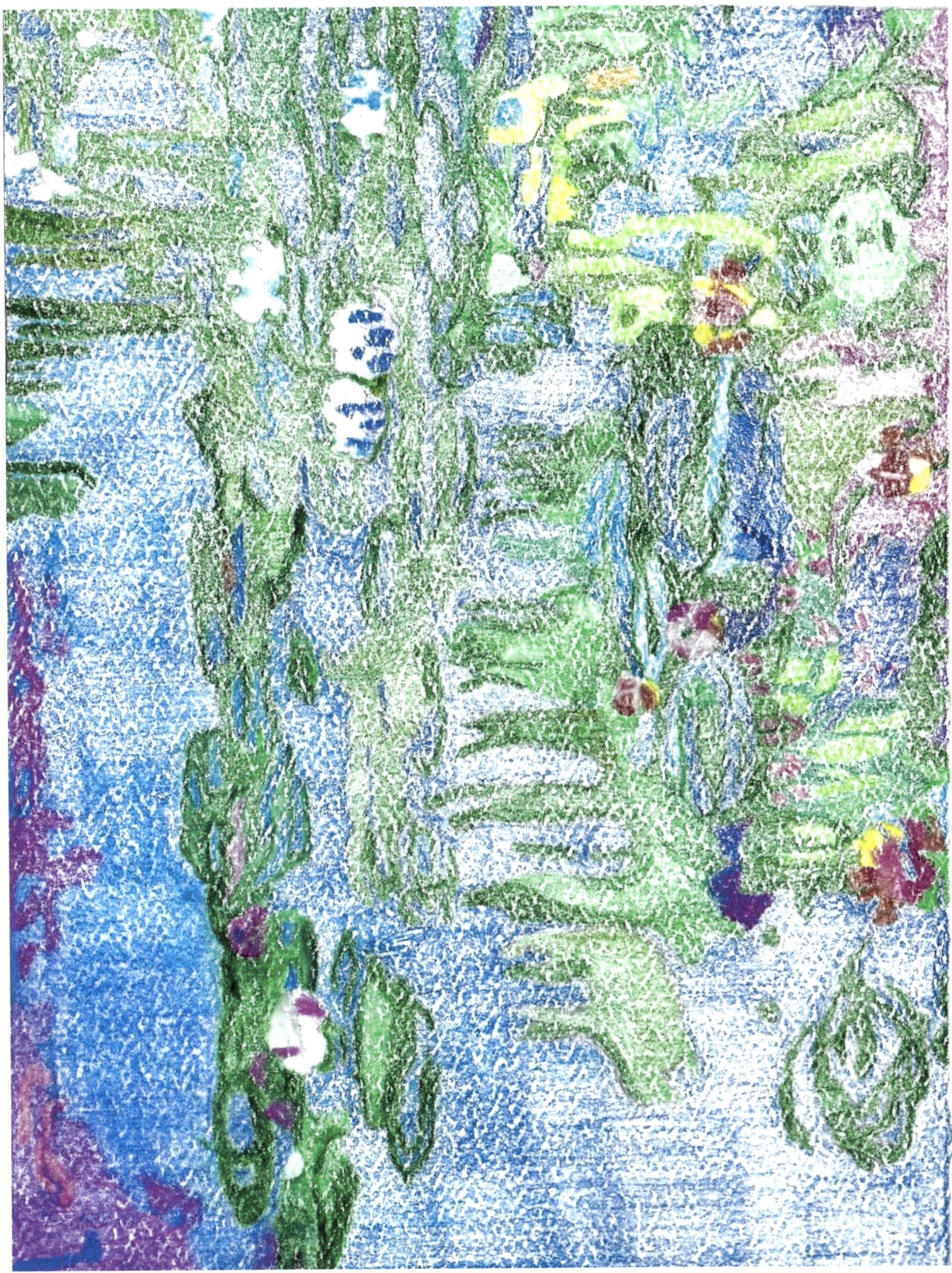

Pablo Picasso So Great, Not So So

Pablo Picasso so
great, not so so
Most famous artist
of the era we're in
Painted acrobats and
the *Harlequin*

Born in Spain but lived in France
Fascinated by dreams and unconscious trance
A child prodigy at age 14
He began to paint, realism was seen

Then a Blue Period for
a few years
Painted in shades of
blue to reflect his tears
Later emotions
warmed and his colors
Showing us circus
scenes and some
monsters

Cubism was born from
his distorted lines
Breaking down subjects
into shapes for designs
There was a war in
Spain, he wanted peace
He created *Guernica*, a
masterpiece

After the war he became
more relaxed
Painted and sculpted, no
moods were taxed
Pablo Picasso so great, not
so so
Most famous artist of the
era we're in
Painted acrobats and the
Harlequin

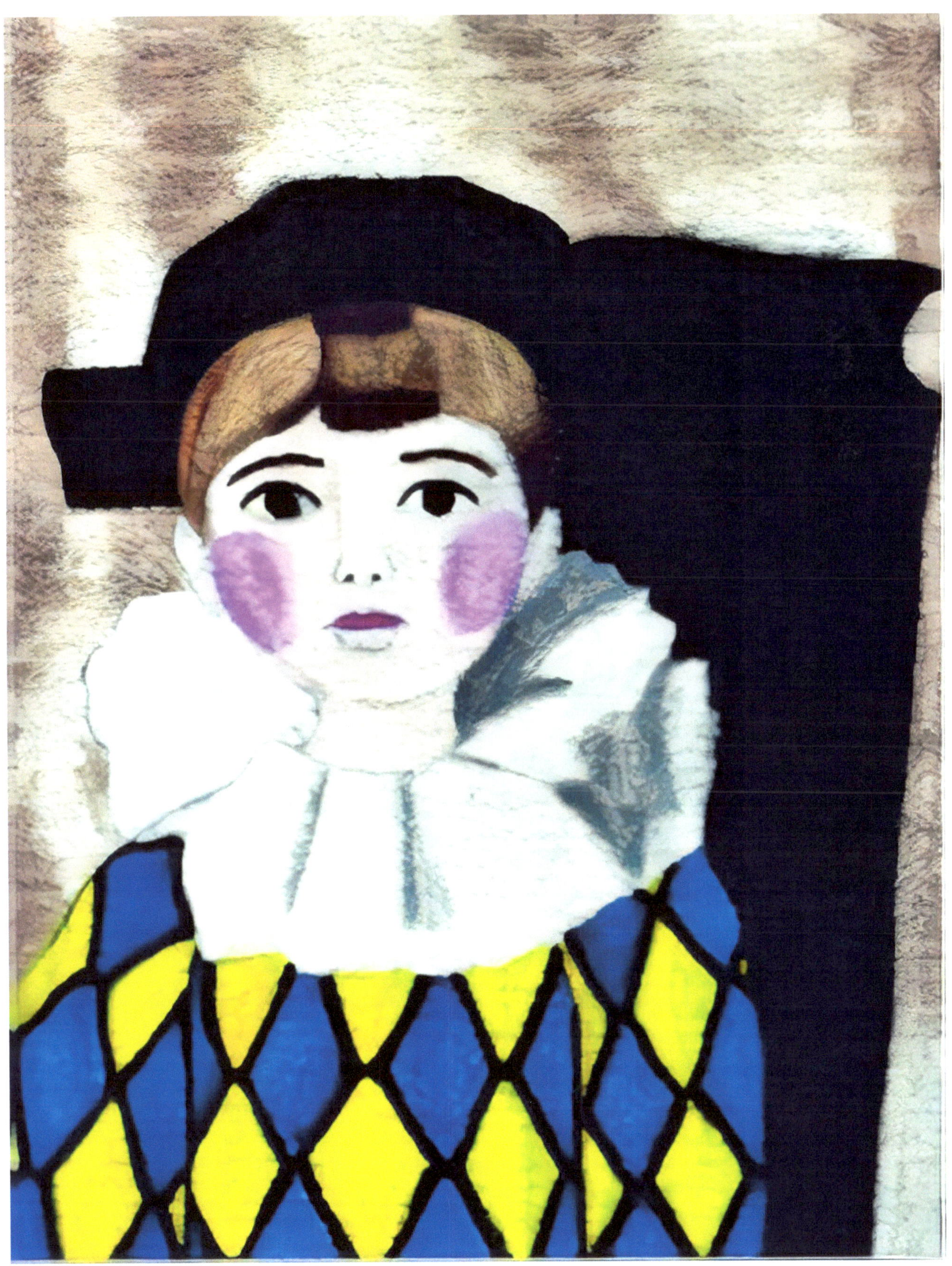

Rembrandt

Was His First Name

Rembrandt

        was his first name

Or did you know?

He painted portraits in Holland 300 years ago

Used mostly dark colors, but his faces they did glow

He really was a master of light and shadow

Painted many people, of course, his own son *Titus*

His love of life and beauty

Through paintings they still guide us

Nightwatch was his most famous depiction

Of soldiers preparing to march

But a major source of friction

Since soldiers commissioned him but they all appeared the same size

The crowded groupings were a surprise!

The death of his loving wife, another tragedy in his life

Of his four children, Titus was the only one to survive

Sad though he was, he continued to paint

The Netherlands' greatest artist he later became

Despite loneliness, losses, and feeling low

Rembrandt

        was his first name

Or did you know?

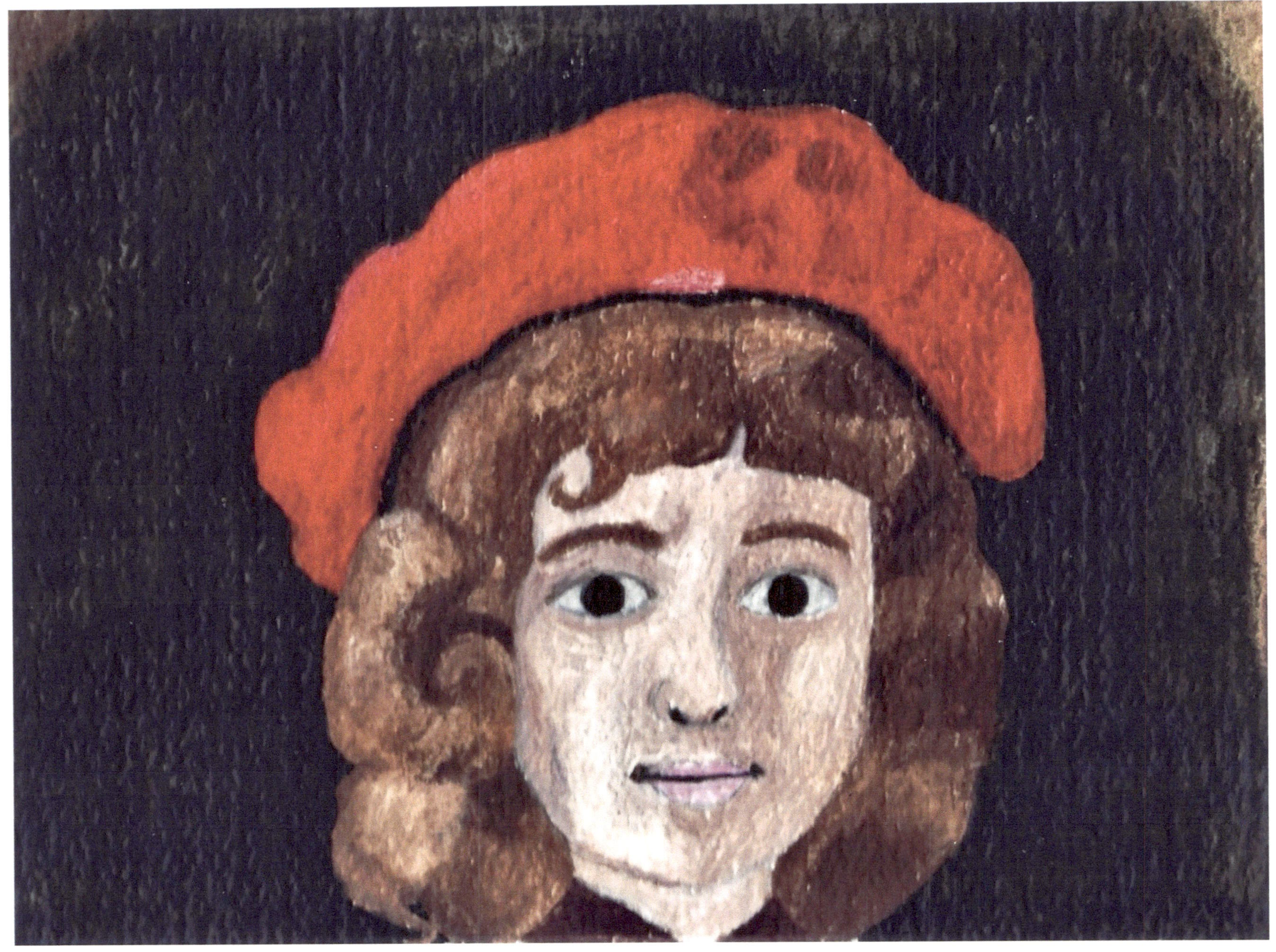

HI, NORMAN ROCKWELL, LET'S WALK DOWN THE STREET

Hi, Norman Rockwell, let's walk down the street
People who you'll paint are people who you'll meet…
So, "How do you do?" We want to meet you:
A scrawny, clumsy child, the opposite of Jarvis your older brother
He, the natural athlete; you, the natural artist, to the chagrin of your mother
Though her father had been a portrait painter and your dad could copy an illustration
Your mom preferred you find a respectable vocation and keep art as an avocation
But you knew you had talent and dropped out of school at age 15
To become a serious illustrator of a book or life scene
Then drawing classes at the Art Students League
Studying the skeleton, sketching live models, ignoring fatigue
Early work included *Tell Me Stories* and *Boys Life* covers
Yes, you were talented as *THE SATURDAY EVENING POST* editor discovers
The success of your first and subsequent 323 covers for the *POST*
Plus scenes from Twain's books, your visit to the actual cave with a ghost?
But your message behind the picture is what mattered most
In your *Daydreams* we relate to the respite we humans seek
Your wistful girl looking melancholic and meek
Sweeping away her troubles or daily grind; "What if…" thoughts filling her mind
Sure, your subjects had feelings, they could think or dream
People saved your covers and anticipated your next theme
What current event, neighbor, or VIP might appear?
Akin to our present day predictions of *Time* magazine's person(s) of the year
I recall my Eagle Scout brothers reading *Boy's Life*, a positive thing to do
And your scout calendars lived in thousands of homes and in our home, too!
Your *Rosie the Riveter* posters and message still, showing women at work with power and will
However, you wanted more than fame; you wanted more than a name
You wanted to make us stop to empathize with the ups and downs we all realize
Your *Look* cover magazine on school integration affected civil rights causes
Such a powerful, timely commentary with no word clauses
Also honored in your *Triple Self Portrait* stamp, your Stockbridge Museum, your art
Your subjects touched our heart; you made us more human, that sets you apart
Hi, Norman Rockwell, let's walk down the street
People who you'll paint are people who you'll meet
A soldier, a doctor, children wishing, a plumber, a barber, a young boy fishing
Your pictures showed us every day life - times of joy, times of strife
Your posters honored FDR's four freedoms of worship, speech, from want and fear
You've made us proud, you've made us cheer
Hi, Norman Rockwell, let's walk down the street…

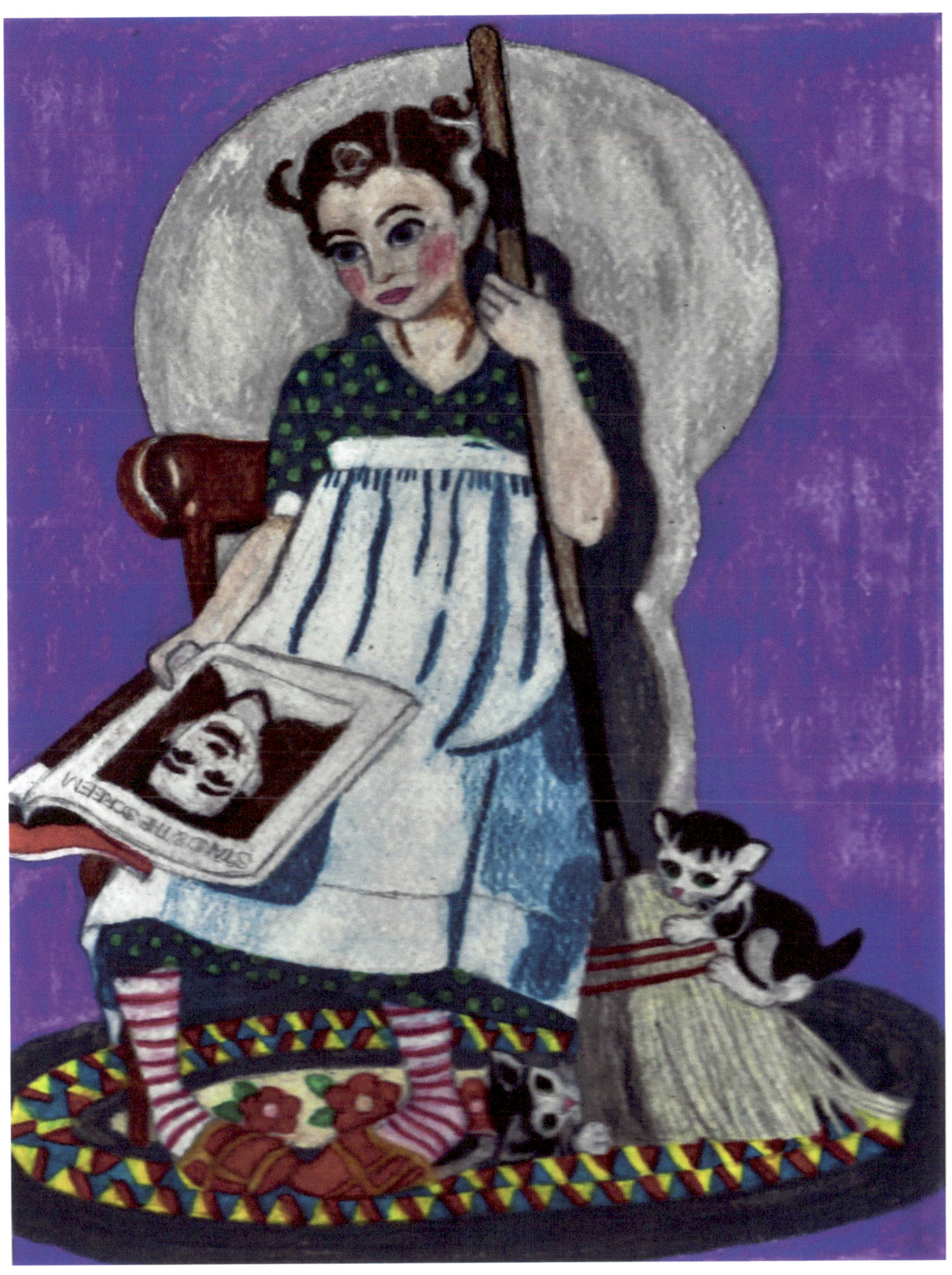
SMOOTHE SCREEN

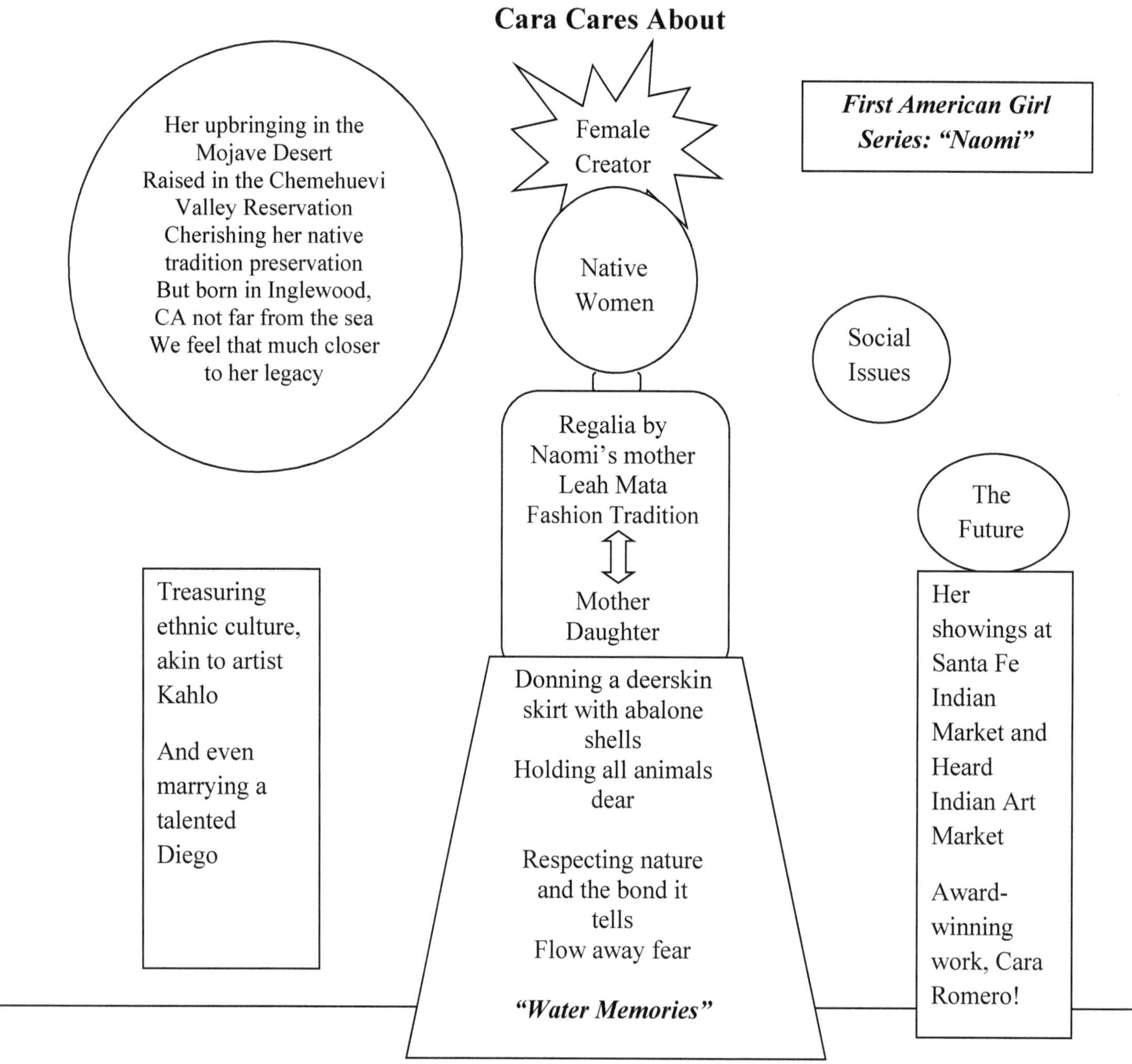

Being indigenous proud
While relating to the current crowd

Communicating through photos
Creating a contemplative scene – theater loud!

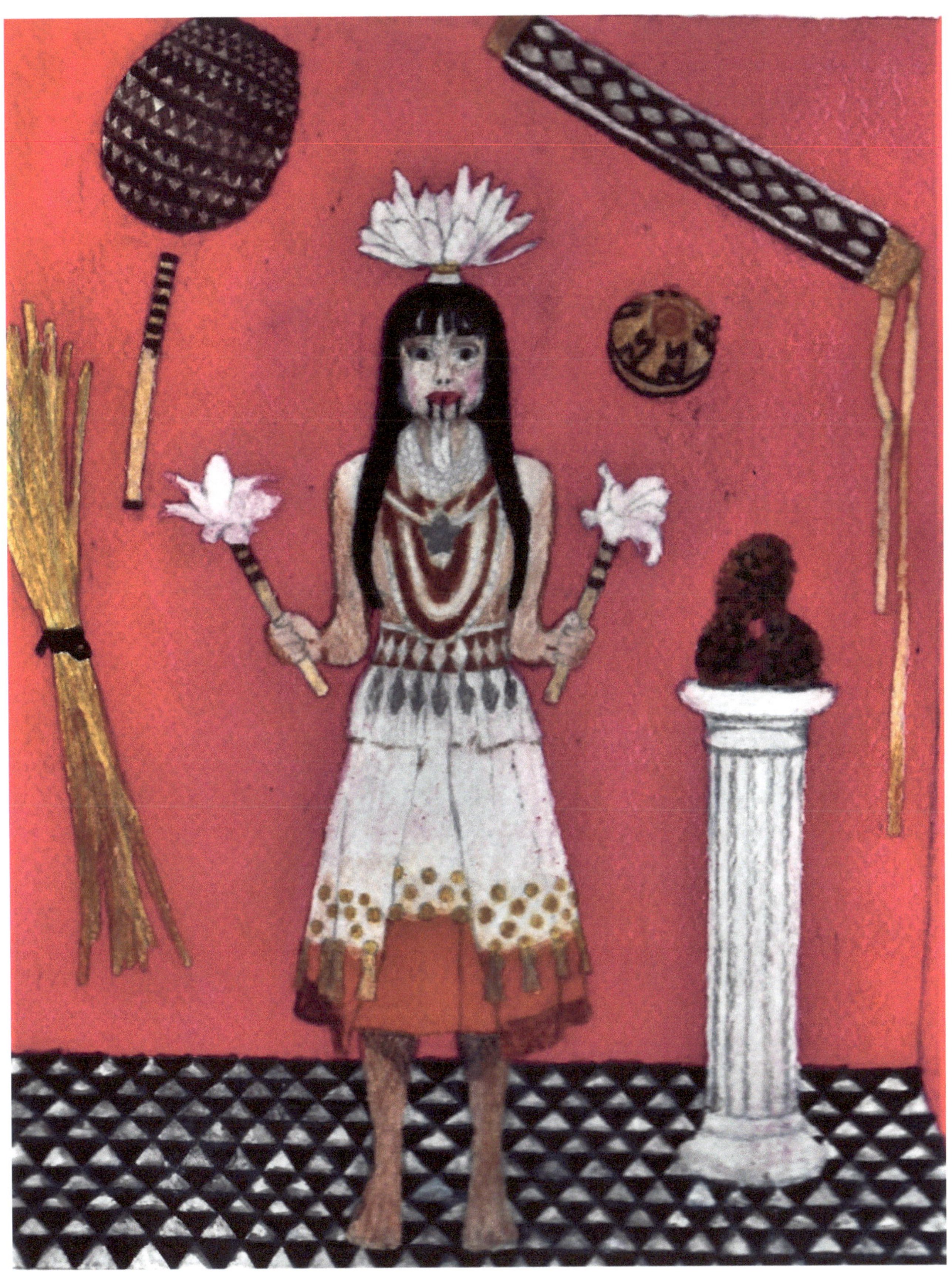

We get the point • Seurat, dot dot

By viewing *Afternoon at La Grande Jatte* •   dot dot

Up close it's difficult to see

Exactly what you meant the dots to be

But at a distance the dots become

Clear subjects, at least to some

The couples, the families, the fisherwoman too

Appear rather like statues brown, orange, and blue

You created your own neo-impressionism style

Making Monet, Pisarro, and other impressionists smile

The myriad, perfect circles from the tip of your brush

Pointillism take patience don't rush

Pointillism made you famous we recall

Many pieces painted but you didn't complete all

We get the point • Seurat, dot dot

By viewing *Afternoon at La Grande Jatte*
dot dot

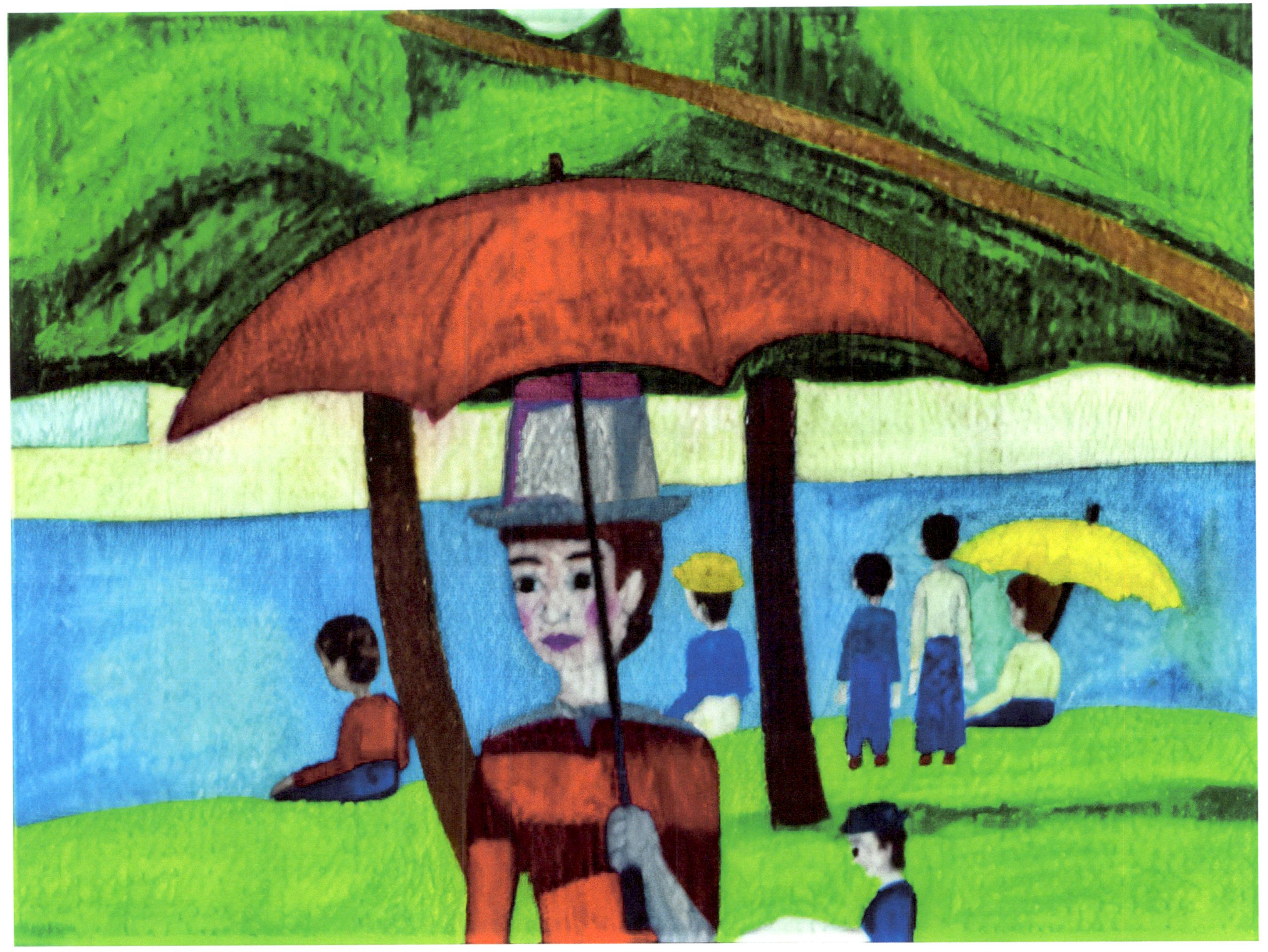

Gilbert Stuart Was an American

TO THE FRONT – MARCH

LEFT   RIGHT

LEFT   RIGHT

LEFT   RIGHT

LEFT

Gilbert Stuart was an American

He painted three portraits of Washington

One's the best he's ever done

He began his art at age thirteen

Studied in London, spent all his money

Returned to the U.S.A., hooray!

President's faces earned him pay

TO THE FRONT – MARCH

LEFT   RIGHT

LEFT   RIGHT

LEFT   RIGHT

LEFT

To replenish his often empty pockets

Stuart counted on Washington's eye sockets

The other odd features he couldn't comprehend

Washington didn't want to be his friend

But Stuart's still a famous person

He painted three portraits of Washington

Two are on display at ***The Huntington***!

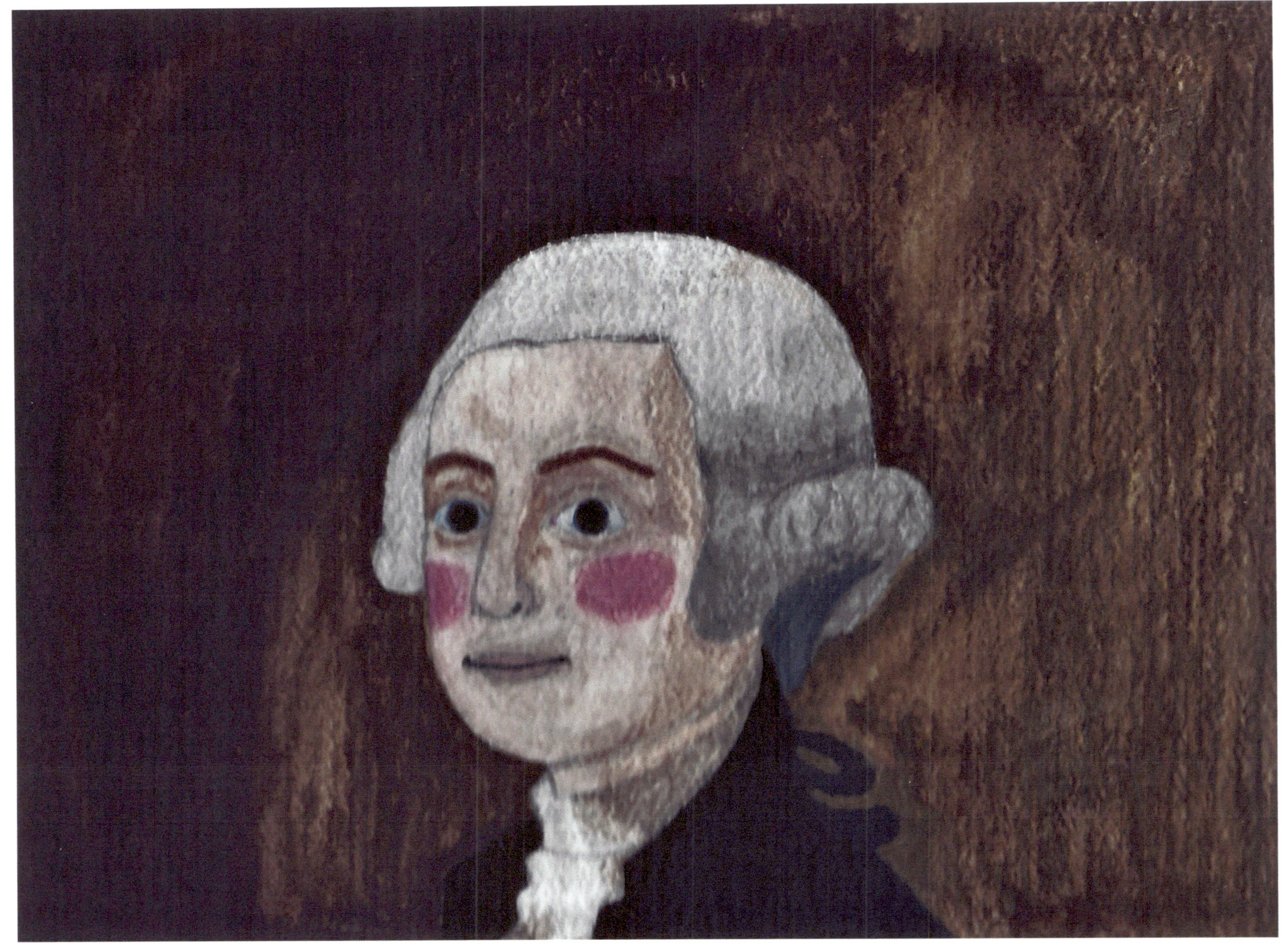

That's a Vincent Van Gogh

That's a Vincent Van Gogh

Short, impressionistic brush strokes- lots of yellow, red, green, and blue

Colors that jump out at you!

Van Gogh, you never let yourself grow old

Possibly because only one of your 1700 paintings ever sold

But now they're worth more than gold!

You were unhappy, emotional, and physically ill

Didn't anyone ever tell you that you were special?

You loved God, nature, people, and many things

And you decided to tell it through your artist's palette

The warm wheat growing in *The Harvest*; the blue quiet of your *Bedroom at Arles*

Lines and greens in *Gauguin's Chair*, the *swirling* and *twirling* of *The Starry Night's* air

Portraits and still lives in those three productive years

Painting all day, talking to Gauguin and Monet all night

No wonder your life was filled with exhaustion and tears

So Dr. Gachet tried to ease your fears

We're sorry no one could make you feel proud, since now your artistic genius rings out loud!

That's a Vincent Van Gogh

Short, impressionistic brush strokes- lots of yellow, red, green, and blue

Colors that jump out at you!

That's a Vincent Van Gogh

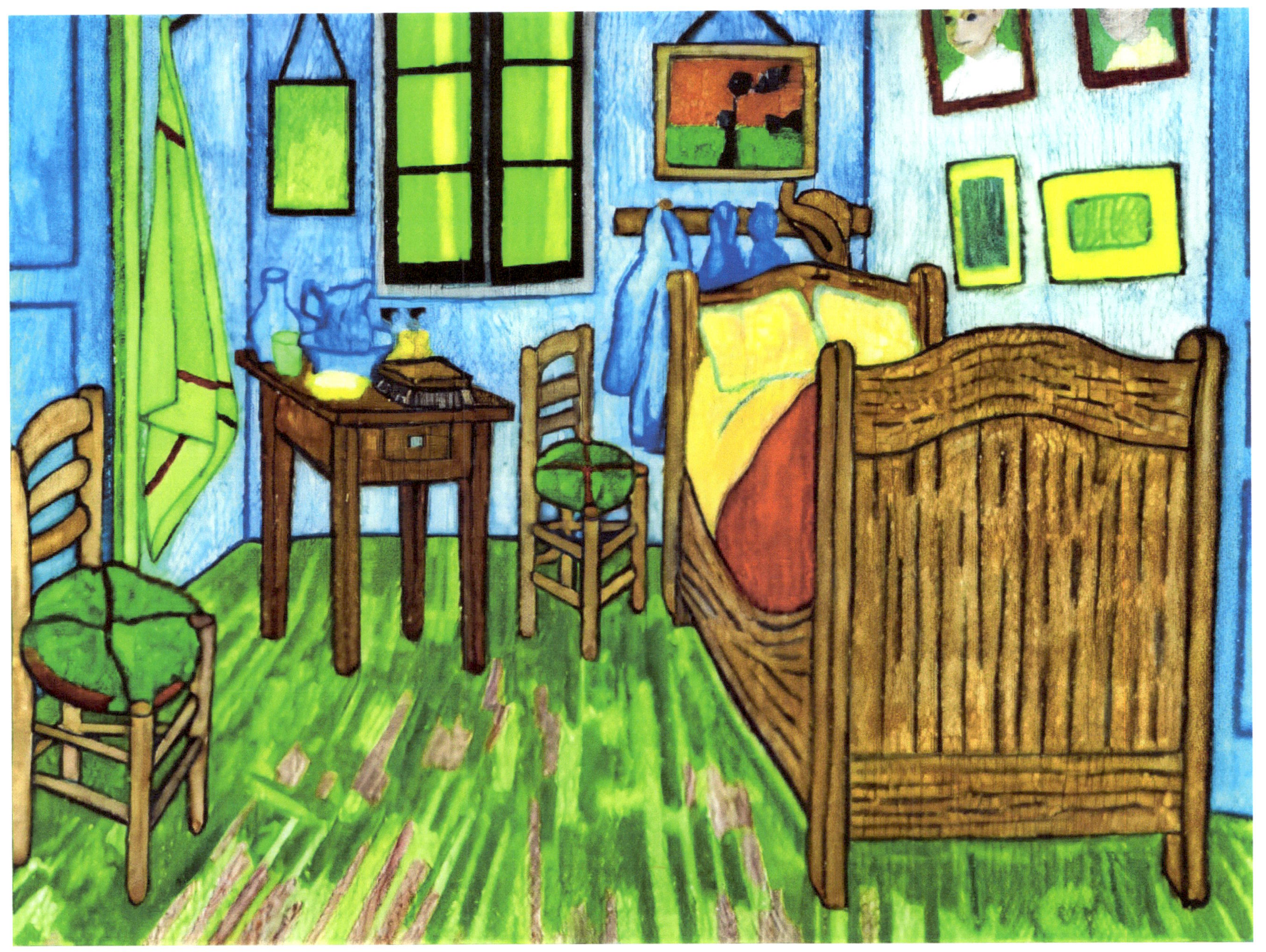

Can it, Warhol! Yes, you can!

A sickly child you spent a great deal of time in bed
Enjoying the comics and movie magazines you read
Early on you showed an innate talent for art
Encouraged and helped by your mom who knew you were smart!
Your teachers suggested weekend art classes at Carnegie Museum of Art
After high school study of illustration at the Carnegie Institute of Technology
Your blotted line-look style was you unique process and methodology
After college first job at *Glamour* magazine drawing shoes
Then a series of ads for a big shoe store, you had nothing to lose!
So you canned your successful career as an illustrator
In hopes of becoming a serious artist later
Tried styles of pop art, a new rage, but you wanted to be unique and turn the page
You needed an idea, so to that end you consulted your interior designer friend
She asked what you really adored
"Money", you replied – maybe she was floored!
But she encouraged you to paint out
And to find something so familiar people forgot about
You gave it thought and found a soup can
Of which many were a childhood fan
Campbell's tomato soup a favorite comfort food
Painting not one, but a canvas of them to evoke a mood
Most viewers loving your work appreciating it as just a creative pop art quirk!
Then your Marilyn Monroe, varying colors and features in each piece
Showing those the year she left life for eternal peace…
Then your breaking into more fame and recognition
As you were acclaimed for taking a subject ordinary
And reproduce it over and over to look extraordinary!
Repetition in your life also – your 400 wigs, 20 cats all called Sam
YOU were the current cool collectible cat – Shibam!
Then adventuring to filmmaking and founding the Factory
So people would later view your paintings as more than satisfactory!
Making the tomato soup can and yourself famous with your style
To be pondered and admired for a very long, long while
You can create, you can duplicate
Yes, you can!
Yes, you can!
Yes, you can!
Yes, you can!
Can it, Warhol!
Yes, YOU can!

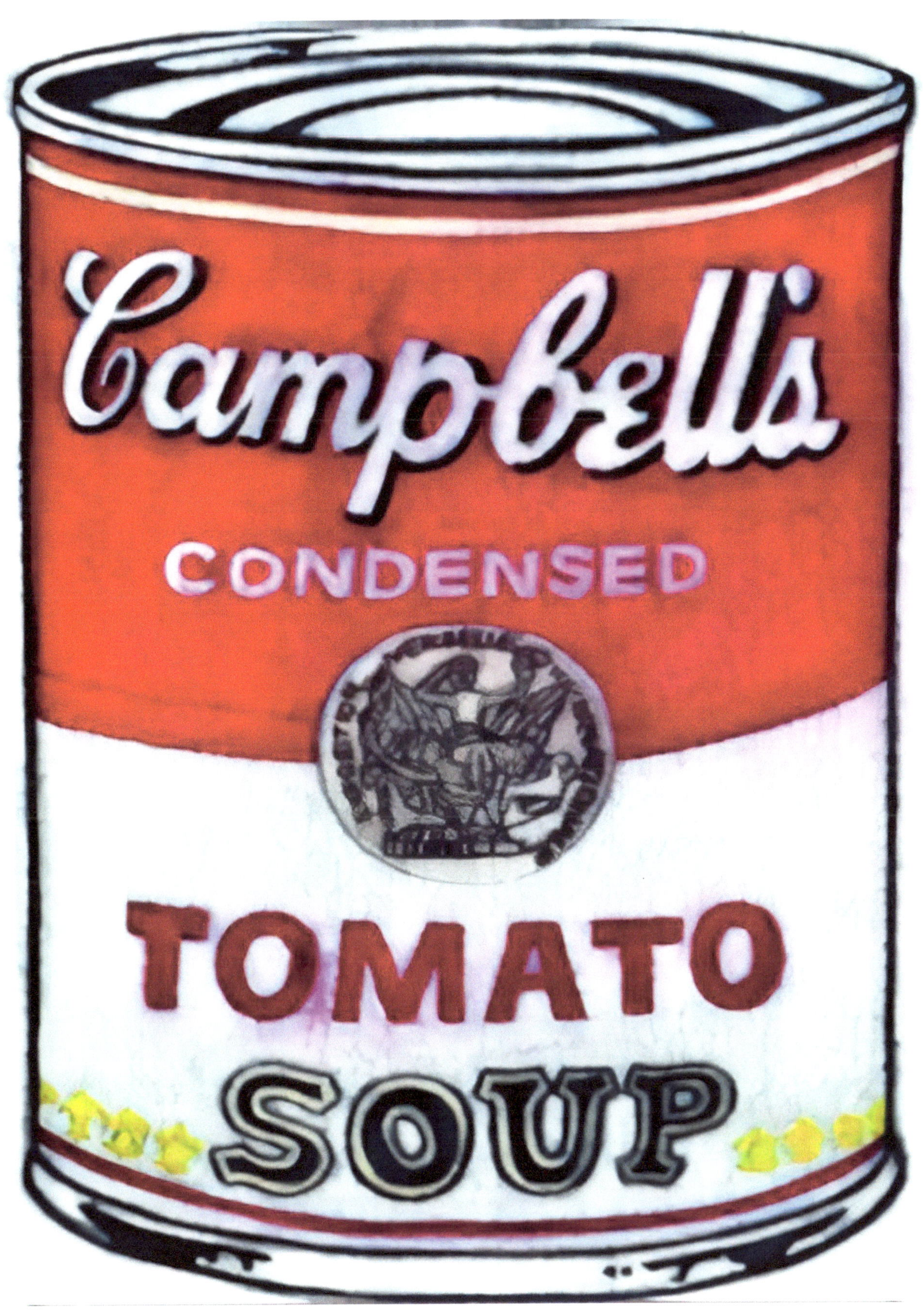

Campbell's
CONDENSED
TOMATO
SOUP

Heidi Dong is So Beautiful, So Beautiful

Fascination with art at a very young age
Then dancing lessons at a later stage
Your talents that family and teachers would nurture
For your rewarding and flourishing future
Plus after-school classes in art, dance, and speech
Then Ready, Willing, and Able where I could meet you and teach
Your brilliant ballet spotlight solos graced us
Your many pique turns and graceful arms in 4th position amazed us
Your colorful, gorgeous costumes with tutus full
      So beautiful, so beautiful!
Plus your paintings in this book and your others, we hail
Your ***Brant Point Lighthouse*** shows us every tiny detail
All because of you and your artistic genius
      So beautiful, so beautiful!

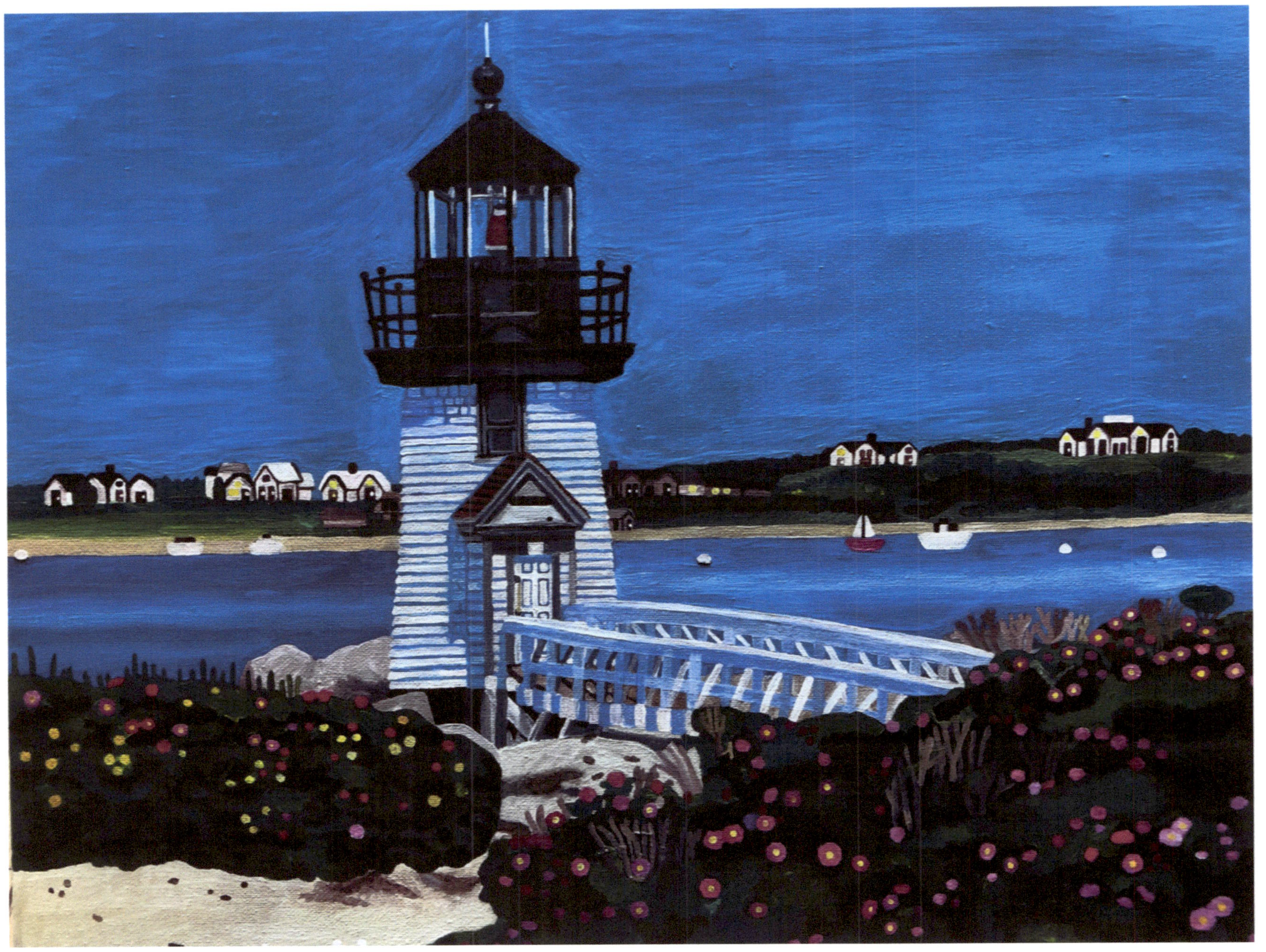

About the Illustrator
Heidi Dong

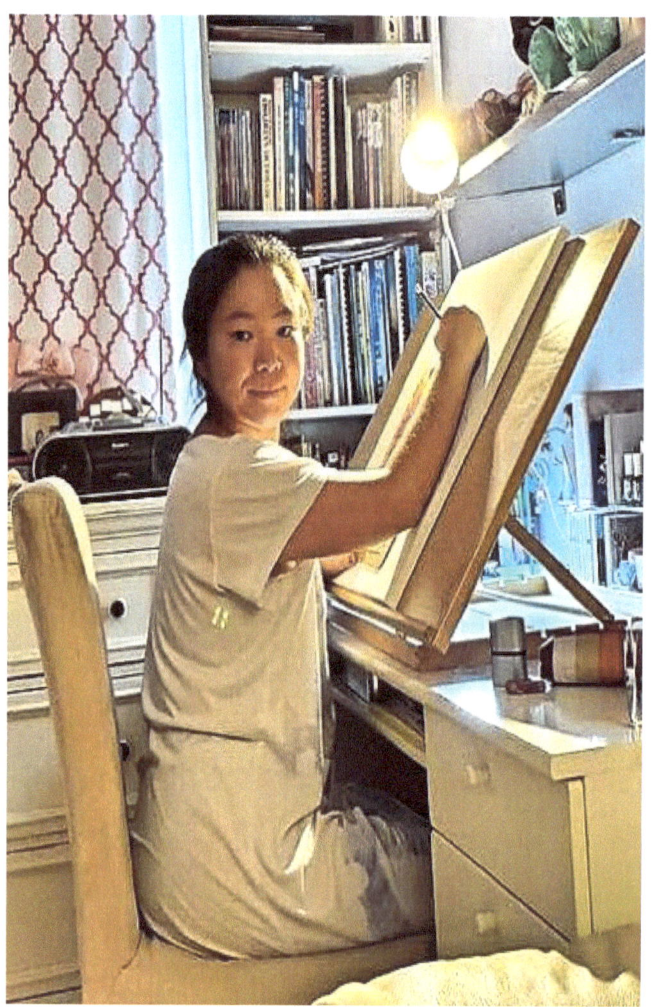

Heidi Dong was born in Torrance, California on January 14, 1991. Her loving Korean parents wondered how their baby with autism would blossom. In a short while, the answer was clear. At age two, she showed no interest in toys or games, preferring art supplies and canvases. She continued her passion for art through school years and beyond. She also began dance lessons at an early stage where her additional artistic abilities were recognized. During high school, she joined Elizabeth Cantine's Ready, Willing, and Able (RWA) Dance Program for students with special needs. Heidi takes these weekly classes at the Palos Verdes Performing Arts Conservatory under the instruction of current director Julie Hast. There, she is able to study many genres of dance and to be assisted by the staff and one-on-one student mentors. She continues to study ballet privately with Liz. In the bi-annual performances at the Norris Theatre, Heidi's performing talents shine in the group dances and in her spotlight ballet solos. Through her weekday Easterseals Program, she works one day a week at Cabrillo Elementary School where she assists Miss Barbie and staff making charts, graphs, and sample patterns. Heidi's printing is more refined than typed font! She also enjoys ICAN summer camp activities including horseback riding, swimming, and hiking. Year-round, she participates in speech and dance classes. She is currently studying art at the Exceptional Children Foundation's Art Center and summer studio. Heidi is able to interpret paintings and photographs as well as replicate most ballet variations that interest her. Her artistic giftedness is truly so beautiful, so beautiful…

Special Thank You

Heidi's dances are beautiful

Heidi's paintings are beautiful

Ms. Liz thanks Heidi

For making her book and her life so beautiful, so beautiful!

About the Author
Elizabeth Cantine

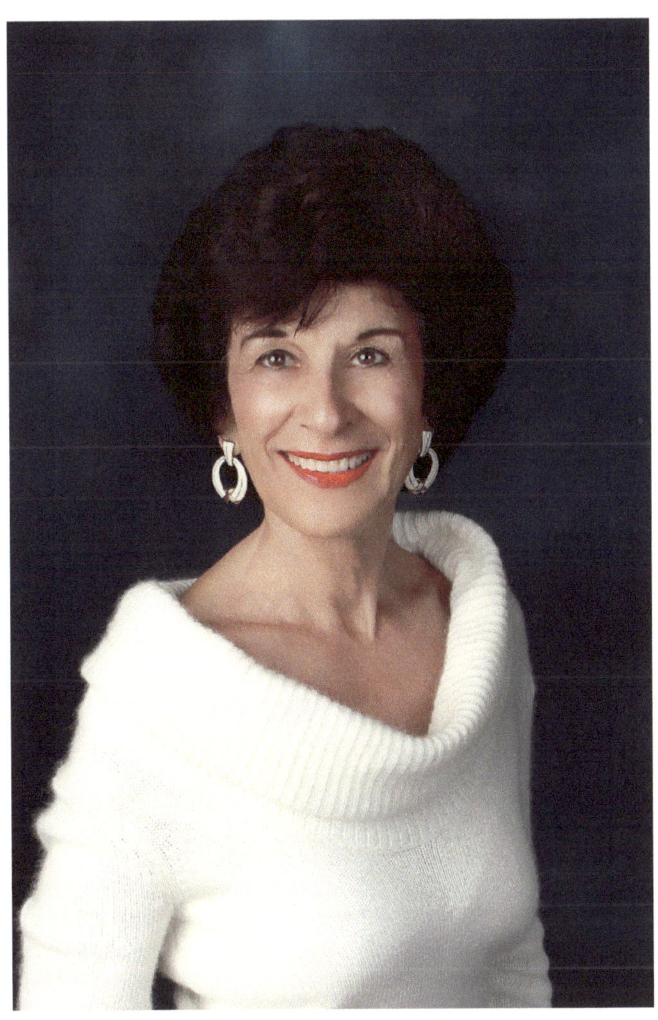

Elizabeth (Liz) Michele Cantine, a graduate from UCLA, has spent her career of over 50 years as a classroom and dance educator. She has written and presented many units integrating the fine arts into the K-12 curriculum. She was an LA Music Center Arts Education Bravo Award Finalist and has served as President of California Dance Educators Association. As Dance Drill Team Coach at Dana Middle School in San Pedro, California, she discovered and taught the awe-inspiring Misty Copeland, first African-American Principal Ballet Dancer at American Ballet Theatre. After retiring from Los Angeles Unified School District, Liz was the Outreach Coordinator for the Carpenter Performing Arts Center, Musical Theatre West, and the Norris Theatre. Later, Liz became the Dance and PE mentor in Palos Verdes Peninsula Unified School District. She also had the opportunity to teach dance in Adaptive PE at Palos Verdes Peninsula High School. The students and parents motivated her to begin an afterschool dance program at Palos Verdes Performing Arts (PVPA) Conservatory for students with special needs. Recognizing the incredible talent of these enthusiastic students, she called the program Ready, Willing and Able (RWA) – life changing for all! She continues to teach privately to some RWA students and group classes to fellow adult dancers. As a former professional dancer and choreographer, she performs with her adult Tap Happy troupe at community venues and outreaches. She also dances with Anne Destabelle's Pennyroyal Players who donate all proceeds to charities. Liz's first published book **Graceful Gratitude – A Book of Holiday Graces** consists of her original poems for major holidays plus a week of daily graces. Now, she is very excited about her second book and the opportunity to share her poetry and to showcase Heidi's artistic abilities in **Brush of Giftedness.**

Liz can be reached via email at *dancinliz@aol.com.*

Quotable Quartet

The Quotable Quartet is comprised of four of Elizabeth Cantine's private dance students with special needs. They are excited about dancing to several of the poems recited by Elizabeth and featured in *Brush of Giftedness*. The Quotable Quartet integrates their multiple intelligences and their individual giftedness making pictures, words, and learning come to life.

Please enjoy these compilations of poems, group dances, and solos entitled "Brush of Giftedness Quotable Quartet" on YouTube. Thank you to Palos Verdes Performing Arts who generously enabled the Quotable Quartet to film on the Norris Theatre Stage.

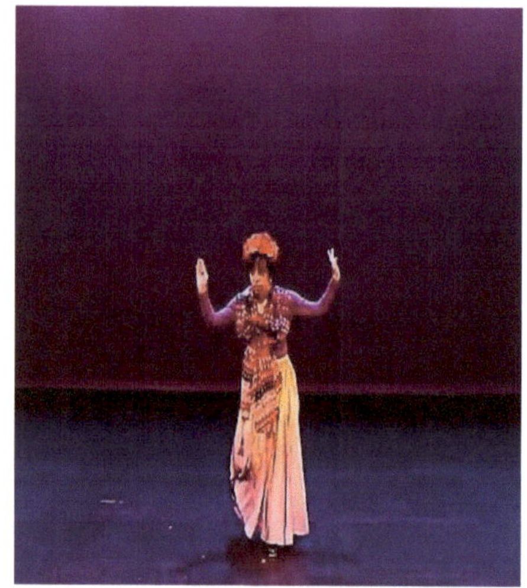

Dahlia

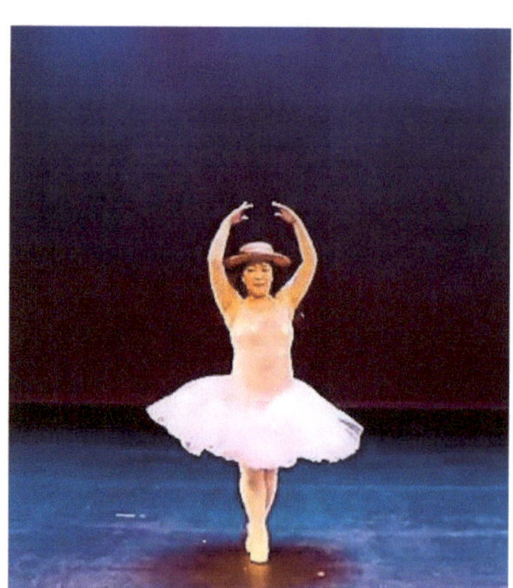

Heidi

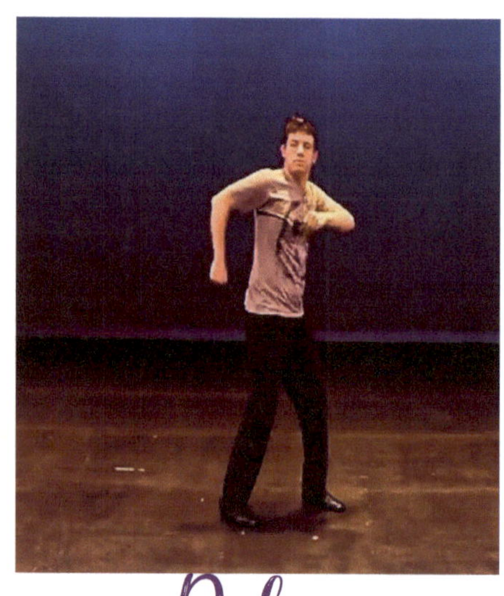

Dylan

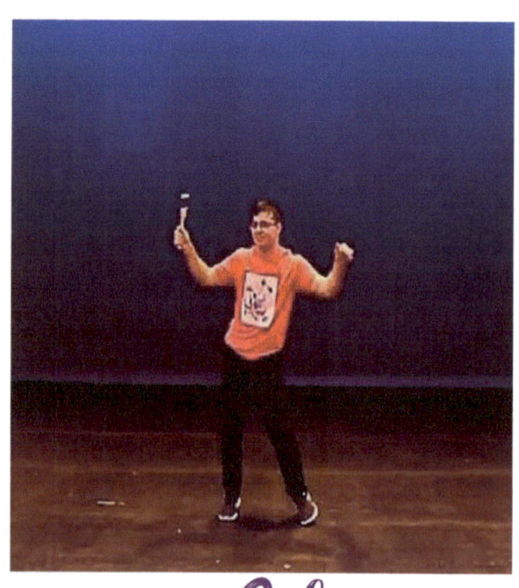

Cole

Acknowledgments

To my beloved parents who appreciated and showed me the power of poetry, art, and dance

To my husband Richard Cantine for all he does so I can pursue my passions

To my son Tom, Miranda, and grandchildren Sophie, Aidan, and Maya for their advice

To Michelle Yamakawa whose talents and technical expertise have made this book a work of art

To my Quotable Quartet, their parents, all my students and friends who brush up my life

To Ready, Willing, and Able (RWA), who will always dance in my heart:

      In Memoriam to Dick and Joan Moe for giving us studio space and the Norris Theatre

      Julie Moe-Reynolds, Palos Verdes Performing Arts (PVPA) Executive Director

      Greg Forbess and PVPA tech staff for videoing the Quartet on the Norris Theatre stage

      Joel Sluyter, PVPA Conservatory Director, for professionally recording all my poems

      Parent founders: Sanaa Abuyounes and Hiromi Ashmore

      Original students: Dahlia, Elena, Maggie, Eva, Andy, and remembered RJ

      Original mentors: Lauren Yamakawa, Sam McPherson, and Kelsey Fung

      Director Julie Hast, staff, and beloved Mr. Dwain Roque

      My private students: Dahlia, Elena, Heidi, Dylan, Tristan, Ian, Maggie, Sergio, and Holly

To my ballet and Quotable Quartet Mentors: Rena Koyama, Brianna Li, Michelle Yamakawa, Kate Hendrick, Aeris Ma, Bailey Kang-Illescas, Devin Reid, Ms. Mary Kay, and Ms. Mastan

To Palos Verdes Library District for displaying our art and poetry

To Michael Sprengel, video producer from PVHS "Live from 205" program

To my gracious friends Maureen Nunn and Adrienne Short for hosting book signings

To my generous Bravo friends for their continual support and donations

To Deborah Paul, author and contributing writer for her feature article in *Peninsula News*

To Anne Destabelle and the Pennyroyal Players for their talents and generosity

To you who educate, create, and think uniquely to make a difference in the world

Preview of Liz's next collaboration…

A new collection of original poems and paintings of famous dancers including her goddaughter Misty Copeland is coming soon.

(first lines of)
The Mystique of Misty

From the very first stance
I knew you were destined to dance
At age 13 trying out for Dana Drill Team
Captain
In awe of just the way you stood
A dancer's alignment and aura you
understood!
She's "the one in a million" –
you could, you would!

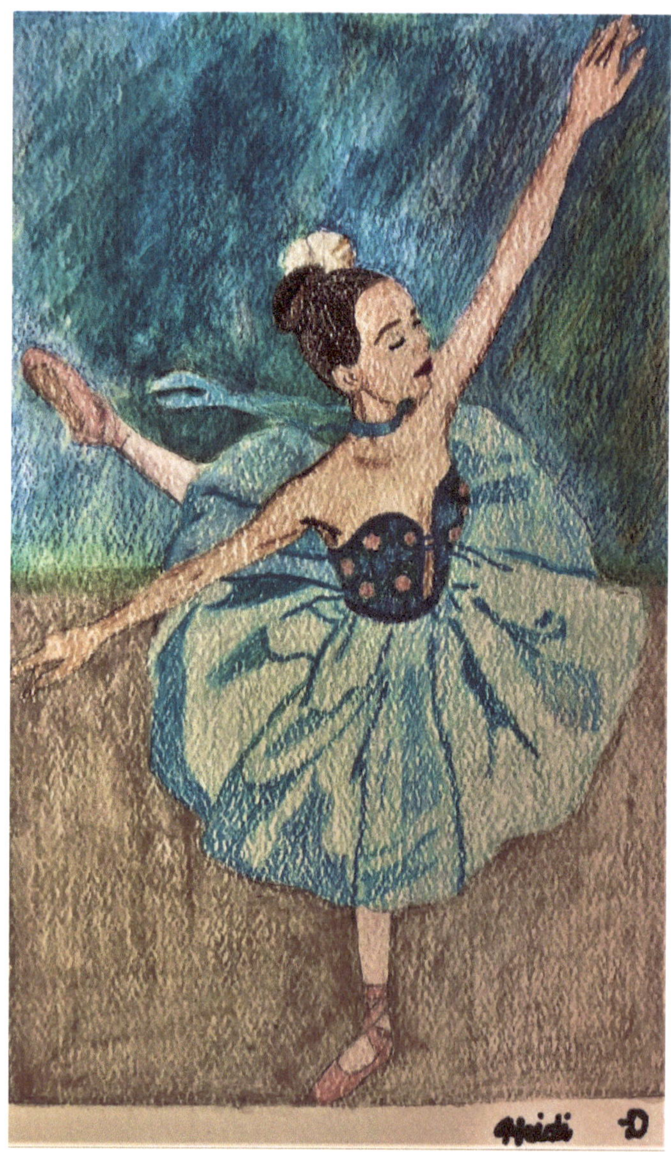

4ARTS EDUCATION PRESS

Brush of Giftedness

Elizabeth Michele Cantine

No part of this publication may be reproduced in whole or in part, or stored in a retrieval system, or transmitted in any form or by any means, electronic, mechanical, photocopying, or otherwise, without written permission of the publisher. Request for permission to make copies of any part of this book should be submitted to dancinliz@aol.com.

Hardcover Edition: ISBN-13: 978-1-7321163-1-3

Library of Congress Registration Number: TX 8-892-557

Printed in the USA

www.ingramcontent.com/pod-product-compliance
Lightning Source LLC
Chambersburg PA
CBHW042204030726
47602CB00007B/119